Bible Answers to Man's Questions On

DEMONS

Volume 4 of the Satan, Demons, and Demon Possession Series

By Kenneth E. Hagin

First Printing 1983

ISBN 0-89276-028-1

In the U.S. write:
Kenneth Hagin Ministries
P.O. Box 50126
Tulsa, Oklahoma 74150

In Canada write:
Kenneth Hagin Ministries
P.O. Box 335
Islington (Toronto), Ontario
Canada, M9A 4X3

Contents

Foreword

Bible Answers to Man's Questions
on Demons . . . . Pages 1 — 28

The Satan, Demons, and Demon Possession Series:

Volume 1 — *The Origin and Operation of Demons*
Volume 2 — *Demons and How To Deal With Them*
Volume 3 — *Ministering to the Oppressed*
Volume 4 — *Bible Answers to Man's Questions on Demons*

Foreword

This is the fourth book in our series on the subject of demonology. In these days, knowledge will increase concerning dealing with demons. Even now we can see the beginning of a new move in this area.

Our first book, *The Origin and Operation of Demons,* deals with the creation and fall of Satan and his angels, and shows how they operate in the earth today.

Second in our series is *Demons and How To Deal With Them.* This book shows how demons indwell man's spirit, and explains how to deal with evil spirits.

The third book, *Ministering to the Oppressed,* deals in depth with the operation of the gift of discerning of spirits, and with ministry to those suffering from various forms of demonic oppression.

This fourth book, *Bible Answers to Man's Questions on Demons,* contains some of the most-asked questions on Satan and evil spirits. Answers are given in light of the Word of God.

This book is an overview, highlighting key topics concerning demons. Answers are given to questions such as, "Can a Christian have a demon?" and "Does the presence of sickness and disease always indicate demonic activity?" These are intended to help equip students of God's Word in the fight against powers and principalities arrayed against them.

Thank God, when we learn our authority, and when we learn what the Word of God teaches concerning dealing with demons, we do have victory over the devil in any situation.

Kenneth E. Hagin

Tulsa, Oklahoma
July 1983

Question: Can a Christian have a demon?

Answer: There is no such thing as a Christian's being demon possessed. *To be demon possessed means to be completely taken over — spirit, soul, and body — by the devil.* This was the case with the madman at Gadara (Mark 5).

Of course, if a person backslides, he's over in the devil's territory. By yielding to the devil, he could be taken over. But there is no such thing as a Christian's being demon possessed, even though he might not be walking in the best fellowship in the world. (Some people may not be walking in the best fellowship, but they're walking in all the light they have.)

A Christian, on the other hand, can be *oppressed.* All the demons I've dealt with in Christians have either been in the body or the mind. You'll find that's where their activity is.

A person could backslide and deliberately walk away from God, and the devil could eventually take over his spirit. *But a Christian walking with God can't be taken over by the devil.* In fact, the devil can't do anything in him without his permission. The Bible says, *"Neither give place to the devil"* (Eph. 4:27).

Something we need to realize is that there are degrees of oppression and possession. If you have received the baptism of the Holy Spirit, you can say, "I have the Holy Spirit." But how much of *you* does the Holy Spirit have? You can be halfway or fully yielded to Him. The same is true concerning oppression. You can be halfway or fully yielded to the devil.

Question: Does the presence of sickness and disease always indicate demonic activity?

Answer: The devil is behind all sickness and disease, but that doesn't mean there is the literal presence of an evil spirit in a person. Scripture tells us Jesus "...*went*

1

about doing good, and healing all that were oppressed of the devil.... " (Acts 10:38). He didn't just single out certain ones and say that they were oppressed, because the Bible teaches that all sickness is oppression of the enemy.

But sometimes there is the literal presence of a spirit there. In some cases a demon that brought a certain sickness may remain in the body and enforce sickness, so that demon has to be dealt with.

Question: Should you talk to demons when calling them out?

Answer: When Jesus appeared to me in a vision in 1952 to teach me about the devil, demons, and demon possession, He told me this: "When you get into the presence of those who are fully demon possessed, from this moment forward they will recognize you like they did me when I'd go into the Temple. They'd cry out to me, 'We know thee, who thou art.' But don't let them talk."

Did you ever notice that Jesus would tell them to be quiet? There's no Scripture in the New Testament where He ever held a conversation with demons. He told me, "From this night forward, through either the word of knowledge or discerning of spirits, you will know what kind of spirit a person has, and you can call him out."

There are many kinds of spirits. There are deceiving spirits, lying spirits, religious spirits, homosexual and lesbian spirits, deaf and dumb spirits, and many more. And I'll tell you the truth — some of those spirits smell. The homosexual spirits smell the worst. I've walked into a room and have known there was somebody there with a homosexual spirit; and I have known who it was in. I also can tell when the spirit of death is on somebody. I can smell it sometimes.

Jesus told me in the vision, "To cast demons out, you sometimes (but not always) need to know what kind they are. First, tell a demon to come out, and if he doesn't, ask how many there are.''

You remember when Jesus was casting demons out of the Gadarene demoniac He asked, "What is thy name?" The answer, "Legion," involved both name and number.

Question: Can a person be possessed by more than one demon?

Answer: No, only one evil spirit does the possessing. When Jesus went to the country of the Gadarenes, the Bible tells us "*. . .immediately there met him out of the tombs a man with an unclean spirit. . . .*" (Mark 5:2). Notice the Scriptures say "spirit" (singular). Now verse 15 tells us, "*And they come to Jesus, and see him that was possessed with the devil, and had the legion. . . .*"But you see, all those demons didn't possess that man. Only *one* of them possessed him. He wasn't possessed with 2,000 devils, or a legion. The others were in there, but only one of them possessed him.

Question: Can the devil see what we're doing?

Answer: I was once holding some meetings in South Texas, and a church in a nearby town was between pastors. The board asked if I would preach for them for about ten days after I finished my meetings. I told them I would, and they assured me they would reserve a room for me at a certain motel.

When I arrived at the motel, the main deacon of the church called me and said, "Brother Hagin, I hate to bother you, but you know something about dealing with this kind of thing. My son, who is 37 years of age, is on drugs and alcohol."

He explained that the young man would go wild and wouldn't stay home, but he'd come back once in a while. Mostly he just wandered around. He didn't have any home, and he never had been married. When he would come back, his parents would try to help him, but he'd throw spells and break furniture. He had returned that day and was having some kind of spell. He may have been high on drugs.

This deacon said, "I don't know what to do. I hate to have my own son arrested." I told him I would go to see him.

When I got to their house, the son was sitting on the couch. I never had met him. He was in disarray, his hair was standing up on end, and he was holding his head in his hands, moaning. He looked up and said, "I know who you are! I saw you when you came into town this afternoon. I saw you when you came down such-and-such street. I saw you when you turned."

I said, "Yeah, I know you know me and you know I've got authority over you. Now you shut up! Shut up in the Name of Jesus!"

The devil in him had watched me come to town. But, thank God, we have authority over every demonic spirit in the Name of Jesus. We have nothing to fear.

Question: When dealing with demons in a person's life, what is the next step once the person has been delivered?

Answer: When a person is delivered from sin, from sickness, from the devil, or from anything, he immediately needs to be pushed into the discipline of confession, testimony, and service.

We can follow the example of Jesus. Mark 5 tells how Jesus went with His disciples across the Sea of Galilee to the country of the Gadarenes and was immediately met by a lunatic, a man completely possessed by a demon. We can get some understanding of the awful power that had overcome that man by looking at the destruction of the herd of swine after Jesus had delivered him.

The man had been completely delivered. His entire appearance had changed. Before, he had been a wild maniac. Now he was sitting at the feet of Jesus, clothed and in his right mind. He wanted to cling to Jesus, his Deliverer. And he desired to go with Jesus and remain with Him. But the 19th verse of Mark 5 says, *"Howbeit Jesus suffered him not, but saith unto him, Go home to thy friends, and tell them how great things the Lord hath done for thee, and hath had compassion on thee."*

You see, Jesus knew the man needed to be pushed out into the discipline of confession, testimony, and service. So immediately He sent him out to spread the news of his deliverance in his hometown and to his people.

Jesus knew that every advance would give this man new assurance and strength. And before long, the entire region of Decapolis was so stirred by this one man's testimony that the way was prepared for the Lord Jesus, and a mighty work was wrought.

Mark records in his Gospel what happened during Jesus' second visit to the coasts of Decapolis: a great multitude came to hear Him, a deaf and dumb man was healed, and a few fish and loaves of bread were multiplied to feed the 4,000 (Mark 7:31-8:9). Think about the power of that one man's testimony!

Sometimes we must trust young disciples with the boldest and most difficult service. It's good for them. It will make them grow up in a hurry!

I'm not saying that they won't need help and encouragement from more mature Christians, but even baby Christians have authority in the Name of Jesus. God wants people to grow up spiritually so they can stand on their own two feet. He wants them to take their place in Christ, knowing the Name of Jesus belongs to them as much as it does to the preacher or evangelist. They can put the devil to flight!

Question: Do we have authority over others' wills?

Answer: Often we try to take the authority we have in our own lives and exercise it in somebody else's life. But we don't have it. You see, you can run the devil off from your own life, but you can't always run the devil off from somebody else's. I can handle my own finances, but I can't always handle your finances unless you turn them over to me.

Spiritual things are just as real as material or natural things. But when it comes to spiritual things, it seems we think we can intrude into other people's lives without their consent. Sometimes people will act like they're giving their consent, but their heart is not in it. They won't even look you in the eye.

As long as a person's own mentality and will is at work and he can control himself, he has a lot to do with his deliverance. You must teach people their responsibility to agree with you.

If a person's mind is gone — if he's insane — that's a different thing. That's where we have to depend on the Spirit of God to help us. We don't have authority there. That's another "household" — another person.

If we could exercise authority in that area, we could make every sinner in the world get saved! See where we miss it? We take a truth that applies to us and we try to work it in somebody else's life. Did you ever stop to think that it didn't work in your life until you were enlightened and you put it to work?

Question: Will the devil try to return after he has been cast out?

Answer: The devil always will endeavor to go right back to the place he has left. That is a spiritual principle explained for us in Matthew 12:

MATTHEW 12:43,44
43 When the unclean spirit is gone out of a man, he walketh through dry places, seeking rest, and findeth none.
44 Then he saith, I will return into my house from whence I came out; and when he is come, he findeth it empty, swept, and garnished.

If you get saved, the devil will try to get back in your life; he'll try to get you to do wrong. If you were delivered of sickness, he'll try to put the same thing back on you. Matthew 12:45 tells us: *"Then goeth he, and taketh with himself seven other spirits more wicked than himself, and they enter in and dwell there: and the last state of that man is worse than the first. . . . "*

In dealing with demons in the lives of Christians, you must be careful to get the Word into people. Otherwise you'll do them an injustice, because they may wind up seven times worse than what they were.

Question: How much authority do we have to keep devils off our property?

Answer: The Church of the Lord Jesus Christ has more authority than we have realized yet. Demons will not act up as long as they are in my presence; they know I've got authority over them.

Ernie Reb, a missionary to the Philippines, had an incident happen one time involving devils on his property. He had moved to an island that was supposed to be the very stronghold of Satan. He was building a home on the island and was planning to live there.

During the construction, one of the carpenters started hollering, and Brother Reb went to see what was wrong. The fellow was thrashing around like he was wrestling with something. He was yelling, "Get him off of me! Get him off of me!"

Brother Reb said, "I saw something rip his pants leg.

Tooth marks appeared, and the man started bleeding from the hip down. All this time he was hollering, 'Get him off of me!'

"I realized it had to be the devil. I said, 'I command you in the Name of the Lord Jesus Christ, you leave him! This is my property. You've got no right on my property.' " He said the thing ran off. He never did see him, but the other man saw him.

After that the other carpenters became afraid to work there. The witch doctor came, and he wanted to sacrifice a pig and chicken. Their blood was supposed to appease the demons.

Brother Reb said, "No! You won't come on my property! You won't sacrifice anything on my property! There are no evil spirits here. I told them not to come back. They won't come on my property. They won't set foot on my ground. Tell that carpenter to come back. That won't happen again."

You see, those demons knew Brother Reb. The devils know you. They will sit around and laugh at you if you don't exercise your authority.

The witch doctor came back and said to Brother Reb, "If that man comes back to work and the devil jumps on him and kills him, you'll be responsible. He has a wife and several children, and you'll have to take care of them if he's killed."

Brother Reb said, "Tell him to come back. Those devils won't attack him anymore. I have forbidden them to come on my property, just like I'm forbidding you. You're not offering any sacrifices on my property."

The carpenter was off work quite a while, waiting for his leg to heal. He couldn't even walk on it. But eventually he came back and never was attacked anymore. When we boldly resist the devil, he has to flee.

Question: How much authority over the devil do we have when we are in his territory?

Answer: The devil has no right to trespass on God's property. But if you trespass on the devil's property, he's got a right to jump on you. God can't keep him from it, and you can't keep him from it, because you're on his property.

It's like this: I don't have authority in your house or apartment. I can't go there and say, "We're going to move everything out of this room and sell all of it."

In the house of God, if the devil comes around, we've got authority. But if we go to the devil's house and try to exercise authority, he may throw us out.

In the summer of 1954 I was preaching in Oregon and had my family with me. We took a short vacation while traveling to meetings I was holding. On the way home, we stopped in Salt Lake City, Utah, to see the Mormon Temple.

(I had studied the history of Mormonism and the Book of Mormon. I didn't agree with it because it's unscriptural. It doesn't agree with Paul's revelation.)

A guide was showing us around, explaining how the temple had been built. I was listening intently when I heard somebody hit the ground. I didn't turn around because I was listening to the guide. But somebody said, "That man fell." About that time my wife looked around and said, "Daddy, our baby!" (It was Ken, and actually, he was 15 at the time.) He had hit the ground so hard that his shoes flew off. He was lying on his back with his knees drawn up to his stomach and his face working in some kind of seizure.

If you had any spiritual sense at all, you could sense evil spirits when you stepped on the grounds. These were religious demons. They're the worst kind to get rid of. They're the most difficult to cast out of a person. You can get rid of an adulterous or a lustful demon a hundred times faster than you can a religious demon.

So there Ken lay. Instantly the devil gave me all kinds of mental pictures of my preaching deliverance and Ken being in some kind of institution.

The guide said, "That happens very often when I get to the part in my lecture about Moroni" (the angel who supposedly appeared to Joseph Smith). The guide thought it was a supernatural manifestation to corroborate what he had told about. He said, "Just pull that boy back under a tree. He'll soon come out of it."

I turned around, grabbed hold of Ken's arm and said, "Come out of him in the Name of Jesus Christ!" I literally lifted him by his arms, looked him right in the eye and said again, "Come out of him!" I shouted the third time, "Come out of him!" When I said it the third time, the demon came out. It hadn't been in his spirit, but had attacked his body.

Ken straightened up, blinked his eyes and said, "Daddy, Daddy, where am I?"

I said out loud, "Well, we got on the devil's territory and he jumped on you. But the Name of Jesus delivered you. Now let's get off the devil's territory before he jumps on some of the rest of us." We drove down the highway rejoicing over our victory.

Ken began telling his side of the story. He said the last thing he remembered was the guide talking about Moroni. He explained, "I felt something come out of the ground. It got into my feet and then into my knees. When it got up to about my stomach I don't remember anything else."

The power of God does not come up out of the ground. That wasn't the Holy Spirit. And besides, we got rid of it in the Name of Jesus.

Ken said, "Daddy, what if that had happened at school?" I answered, "Don't ever be afraid it will happen again. If you are afraid, you'll open the door to the devil."

You've got authority over Satan, but know this: Don't get on his territory.

Literally speaking, if you go to places controlled by Satan, you *can* get attacked.

Spiritually speaking, if you get into disobedience, you get spiritually over into the devil's territory.

You *can* claim protection, however, and go wherever you have to go.

Question: How do you minister to someone who is insane?

Answer: The treatment of the insane is one of the most important questions connected with the subject of faith. In my experience in dealing with cases of insanity, there isn't one set pattern you can follow.

But there is one thing we must remember: The true remedy for all deliverance — from sin, from sickness, from demons, or from any evil — is the power of Jesus Christ. Paul says in Romans 1:16: *"For I am not ashamed of the gospel of Christ: for it is the power of God unto salvation . . . ."*

In *The Scofield Reference Bible,* the footnote to this verse states that the Greek and Hebrew words translated "salvation" imply deliverance and healing. There is power in the Gospel of Christ to deliver.

In 1953 I was preaching in Dallas, Texas, holding meetings for a pastor who was away on summer leave. I had been telling about insane people who had been delivered. I told how some received deliverance by wearing prayer cloths I had laid hands on. Three people, in fact, received their deliverance at 3 o'clock in the afternoon after wearing the cloths ten days. I don't know why it happened that way, but it did.

I also told about a woman brought to our parsonage

from an asylum. The Spirit of God told me to go stand in front of her and say, "Come out, thou unclean devil, in the Name of Jesus!"

After hearing me tell of these things, a woman came to me and said, "Brother Hagin, my neighbor has lost her mind. She has been committed to an asylum and is waiting the required ten days before admission. She's not saved, and neither is her husband.

"In the past I have tried to get them to come to church, but they've said, 'We're just not interested in things like that.' Yet when people get into trouble and are desperate, they'll do nearly anything. I'm going to see if the husband will let me bring his wife to the morning service."

She talked to the neighbor, and he agreed his wife could come, so this woman brought her. The insane woman acted like a little child, moving around all the time. She'd constantly talk out loud and jump up. Right in the middle of my Bible lesson, she would pop up and say, "I want a drink of water." Her mind was gone. That first day she didn't pay any attention at all.

The second day, before the service was over, I noticed her eyes on me. She sat there and listened intently. The third day she came with a Bible in her hand, and she'd open it and follow me. The fourth day she was taking notes.

Before the ten days were up, she was saved, baptized in the Holy Spirit, speaking in tongues, and her mind was all right. She never had to go to the asylum. I went back five years later, and she and her husband were in church and on fire for God. I never prayed for her, never cast any devil out of her, or laid hands on her. The Word of God did it!

While I was preaching in this same church, another woman told me she had a sister about 30 years old who had been in an asylum since she was a teenager. Doctors had said she would always need institutional care. They'd said she would live and die in the asylum. However, she was allowed to come home, at times, on furlough.

This woman said, "I'll bring her to these day teaching services. She can understand what you're saying."

So she went and got her. The sister sat there and heard the Word. I never prayed for her or laid hands on her. But her mind became perfectly all right as she listened to the Word being preached.

I got a letter from a 38-year-old woman who had spent half her life in a state institution. She said, "Somebody gave me your book, *Right and Wrong Thinking*. Then I ordered some more books." The same doctors who said she would always need institutional care pronounced her well and dismissed her.

The true remedy for deliverance, friends, is the power of Christ. There's no doubt that when dealing with insanity there are sometimes long and severe trials of faith, but God's Word always works.

This woman who was delivered through reading *Right and Wrong Thinking* is now devoting her life to visiting the insane.

She said, "You can't coddle these patients. People used to sympathize with me and make it worse. I'm having great success getting people delivered, but I get tough with them. I say, 'It's up to you.' "

Question: Why do demons want to inhabit human beings?

Answer: Demons are fallen beings and disembodied spirits. To have the widest possible range of expression, they need to operate through the physical. That's the reason they want to embody man. As a second choice, they'll embody animals. When they do embody man, they make man what they are.

Question: Is alcoholism a demon?

Answer: There's no doubt in my mind that alcoholism is a demon. I've had any number of people tell me, "Brother Hagin, when you laid hands on me, an anointing came into me and I was delivered from alcoholism."

One such testimony came from a man who had been an officer in the U.S. Army. He had been in three government hospitals and three private hospitals. "I took the cure for alcoholism," he told me, "and came out drinking."

He was a man nearly 60 years old. He said, "I remembered when I was 13 years old I knew the Lord. I knew the story of the Prodigal Son, so I got down on my knees and prayed, 'Dear Lord, I'm coming home, just like the Prodigal Son of old, and I ask You to forgive me.' "

He said, "I know the Lord took me back. I had peace in my spirit. It felt to me like a 2,000-pound weight rolled off my chest. But my body still was bound with that alcohol demon. I couldn't quit drinking."

A friend invited him to one of our meetings, and he went. He hadn't been to church in years, and he didn't understand what was happening in the service as people lifted their hands and prayed as one, right out loud.

The church he had gone to as a youngster was quiet and conservative. He told me later, "Then you started that healing line and nearly everybody you laid hands on fell on the floor. That startled me. I said to my friend, 'Well, I'm going down there because I need help desperately, but I'm not going to fall like the rest of them!' "

He told me, "The next thing I knew, I was getting up off the floor. I don't even remember falling. Two outstanding things happened to me: First, when you laid hands on me, something like electricity went all over me — warmth went all over me. It was a great spiritual experience. I got closer to Jesus. It made me love Him more. Second, that alcohol demon I was bound with all those years left me.

I've never touched another drop. I've never even *wanted* another drink!'' Thank God for the power of God!

Question: How do you stop demonic activity that is causing believers to hinder the work of the church?

Answer: If anyone is harassing, intimidating, embarrassing, or deterring the ministry of the church, you know that's the devil. You don't have to have discerning of spirits. You don't have to see the devil. You don't have to know it supernaturally. That's just the devil.

Any Christian can put a stop to that kind of activity in the privacy of his own home. You don't have to go out and broadcast it. You don't have to deal with the person. Just say, "You foul spirit that's operating through So-and-so (and call the person's name), embarrassing, intimidating, harassing, or deterring the ministry of the church, I command you to stop in Jesus' Name.''

Believers can unconsciously yield to the devil and be used of the devil. But that doesn't mean they're unsaved or demon possessed. It takes time and experience to learn not to yield to the devil.

Question: What are the most important qualifications for success in dealing with devils?

Answer: If we know God has planned to use us in a certain way, we can prepare ourselves so we'll be more efficient in that area.

You prepare yourself by fasting and praying, by waiting on God, by meditating in the Word, and by living right. There are two things that are important if you're going to deal with devils: (1) You've got to live right. If you don't live right, you won't have any confidence and the devil will laugh at you. (2) You have to have boldness. And you can't be bold unless you know your rights and privileges in Christ Jesus.

Question: Can demons manifest themselves in the physical realm?

Answer: Yes, although we have the authority to stop those supernatural manifestations.

When Dr. Lester Sumrall was building a church in the Philippines in the 1950s, he heard on the radio about a girl who would fight with something nobody could see, though people could see toothmarks and saliva on her. She had to be confined in a jail cell.

Doctors and psychiatrists examining her asked her what had been biting her. She said, "There are two hairy-looking monsters. One is big and the other is small, and they attack me." They were demons manifesting themselves in the physical realm. Of course, she was not a Christian.

Dr. Sumrall got permission to see her. When he first entered the jail cell, the devil supernaturally spoke through her in English, "I don't like you." The devil cursed him, cursed God, cursed Jesus, and cursed the blood.

After Dr. Sumrall got the girl delivered, she couldn't speak a word of English. He had to communicate with her through an interpreter.

The devil had spoken out of her mouth supernaturally. Those toothmarks were real. That wasn't the girl talking in English, saying, "I don't like you." It was the devil. So the devil *can* do some supernatural things. But, thank God, we do have authority over him.

Question: Can a demon affect the atmosphere of an entire church?

Answer: Yes, a demon can hold a church in bondage.

A certain church where I held a meeting was a very difficult place to preach. The people were good people. They loved the Lord. They loved my preaching. But it was tough to preach there. The very atmosphere was hard.

Everything I said seemed to bounce off the wall back into my face.

Some months later I returned to the area to preach a revival at another church. I also went back to this first church and spent some time with the pastor and his family. I spoke at a New Year's Eve watch night service for them. The next day, the pastor's wife asked, "Brother Hagin, can you see any difference in our church?"

I said, "What do you mean?"

She said, "Is it any easier to preach here? What about the pulpit now?"

I said, "There's as much difference as between daylight and dark. It doesn't seem like the same pulpit. It doesn't seem like the same church."

She said, "Get my husband to tell you about it."

The pastor said, "I don't usually tell people about it because they might think I am crazy."

The spiritual world ought to be as real to us as water is to a fish. Yet, many in the church think a person is a fanatic if he touches that world.

"I won't tell everybody," the pastor said, "but I will tell you. I got so concerned. This was the hardest church I ever preached in. The pulpit seemed to hold me in bondage. I knew the people loved me. They supported me well. We had good fellowship with them in their homes. But that pulpit was like a prison.

"I began to fast and pray about it. The seventh day of my fast, I was kneeling on the platform about three feet behind the pulpit when I happened to look directly overhead. The ceiling disappeared."

(Discerning of spirits had come into manifestation. God allowed this pastor to see into the spirit realm. He saw, sitting up in the rafters directly above the pulpit, a huge spirit. It looked like a big baboon. It was as large as a man.)

The pastor said, "I found myself saying to him, 'You're going to have to come down.' The spirit said nothing, but seemed to draw up as if he didn't want to obey. I said, 'You come down in the Name of the Lord Jesus Christ.'

"He fell down onto the pulpit, then jumped to the floor. I said to him, 'You get out of here!' He said nothing, but looked at me as if to say, 'I don't want to.' I said, 'Just march right out of here, in the Name of Jesus.' He marched down off the platform. I marched right behind him. He would go four or five steps, then stop and look at me, almost begging. I would say, 'No, go on.' But he wouldn't move until I said, 'In the Name of Jesus.'

"We went down the aisle that way, stopping every four or five steps. I went ahead of him and held the vestibule doors open. (The spirit could have gone through the doors, of course, but this is what the pastor did.) That thing would not go through until I said, 'In the Name of Jesus.'

"Then I opened the front door. I stepped back and said, 'Move on out.' He stood there. He never said a word, but I could tell by the expression on his face, he was begging to stay. I said, 'In the Name of Jesus,' and he moved.

"He went down the church steps and got halfway out into the yard. Then he stopped, turned around, and looked at me again. I said, 'No, you don't. You go on in the Name of Jesus.'

"He went as far as the curb. I said, 'You'll have to go on. And don't ever come on these premises again.' He stood there until I said, 'In the Name of Jesus.' Then he ran across the street and down the other side about a quarter of a mile. I watched him run into a nightclub. The next night it burned down.

"Ever since, it has been easy to preach here. The people have noticed. They have asked, 'What happened?' But I didn't tell them."

Question: How do you help someone receive deliverance from smoking?

Answer: A man came to me in tears after a night service. He said, "Brother Hagin, you haven't condemned me, but my own heart condemns me. I'm 63 years old. I've smoked cigarettes since I was 12. I want to be free. Can you help me?"

I said, "I certainly can. All you have to do is give me permission to do it."

He said, "I give you permission. I want to be helped."

I laid my hand on his shoulder and said, "In the Name of Jesus, I break the power of nicotine over your life. And I am going to say this by faith: The next cigarette you smoke will make you sick."

He told me later, "I went home that night. Usually the last thing I did before going to bed was smoke a cigarette. I don't know why, but I didn't smoke that night. I didn't smoke the next morning. I did put the cigarettes in my pocket as I left the house."

This man was a truck driver. That morning he picked up a fellow he knew. The passenger was smoking when he got in the truck.

"I never got so sick in my life," the man told me. "I rolled down the window to get some air. Finally, I had to ask him to put out his cigarette."

Question: How can you help a person who is being hindered by the devil from speaking in tongues?

Answer: Demons attempt to hinder people in every aspect of spiritual life. They try to keep people from all the blessings of God.

Christians who have felt too timid to testify or to pray in public have had their tongues loosed instantly in the Name of Jesus.

We always must be sensitive to the Holy Spirit when

dealing with people. In praying for Christians to be filled with the Holy Spirit, for instance, sometimes it is the devil who's holding them back. It isn't always the case, but I am sensitive to the Holy Spirit when I pray with people, and I know when it is.

I knew that it was this way with one woman when she told me how many years she had been seeking. I laid my hand on her shoulder and said, "I rebuke you, foul spirit of doubt. In the Name of Jesus, leave this woman!" Instantly, she started talking in tongues.

This has happened time and time again. I just lay my hands on the person's shoulder, and very calmly, very quietly, sometimes under my breath, I say, "I rebuke every devil that is holding this person." Instantly they lift both hands and start talking in tongues.

Question: Is it necessary to look a demon possessed person in the eye to get him delivered?

Answer: You have to make contact with a person's eyes sometimes before you can get the devil out of him. Sometimes a person's spirit is trying to hide. But you can get hold of his spirit with your spirit and instantly he'll receive deliverance.

Question: Does God tell us to pray that He'll do something about the devil?

Answer: No. The Scriptures say for *you* to resist the devil and he'll flee from you (James 4:7). *You* is the understood subject of the sentence.

Peter says, "Your adversary" (1 Peter 5:8). (Adversary means "enemy, opponent, or one arrayed against you.") Yes, we've got an enemy, an opponent, one who is arrayed against us.

Satan is the god of this world, seeking whom he may devour. Peter's writings were addressed to Christians. The adversary is not walking about seeking how many *sinners* he may devour; it's the *saints* he's after. What are you going to do about it? Stick your head in the sand like an ostrich and pray that he'll go away? Roll over and play dead like a possum?

Some have said, "I'll just write in a request for those TV preachers to pray. I'll write to that Hagin fellow. He's got faith. Maybe if he'll pray, the devil will leave me alone."

No, seriously, we have to take authority over the devil. Thank God we have authority over him. We don't need to get someone else to do something about it.

Peter didn't say in his letters, "Our beloved Apostle Paul is sending out handkerchiefs, and diseases are leaving people, and demons and evil spirits are going out from them. Why don't you write him for a handkerchief?"

No, it isn't necessary for any child of God to write anybody to get a handkerchief, or for anyone to get someone else to resist the devil and he will flee from you. Go back to the fourth chapter of Ephesians. Remember Paul said, *"Neither give place to the devil"* (Eph. 4:27). That means, "Don't you give the devil place in you." It means he can't take any place unless you give it to him, doesn't it? How are you going to keep him from it? *You* resist him and he will flee.

Question: Is it harmful to talk about the devil's power?
Answer: You can give place to the devil by giving him more credit than God. In church, some people give more praise to the devil than to God. Born-again, Spirit-filled people praise the devil more than they do God.

Some people say, "I'll tell you, the devil is here."

At a place where I preached one time, the pastor got up and said, "The devil is here. He's got us all bound up. I don't know how in the world Brother Hagin is going to preach in this kind of atmosphere. We're going to hurry up here — and turn him loose."

When I got up I said, "No, you're not going to turn me loose. I haven't been bound to begin with. I'm already loose! Now it's been said, 'The devil's here.' "

(You see, the more they talked about the devil, the more frightened they got. They had been saying, "The devil's here, the devil's taken over, the devil's got it." The devil, the devil, the devil — that's all they talked about.)

I said, "The devil will come to church more regularly than most faithful saints. But what of it? Jesus is here, God is here, the Holy Spirit is here. Greater is He that's in me than he that's in the world!"

The people started straightening up in their chairs when I started talking about God. I said, "I don't know if Jesus came with you, but He came with me. Even if you didn't bring Him, I did. He's here. What do we care about the devil?"

Before long, they were jumping and shouting all over the place.

Many people talk about what the devil is doing and how he's keeping them sick and unsuccessful. They give the devil dominion over them. But if you'll talk about what God's Word says, the devil will run from you in terror. You have authority because of the Name of Jesus!

Question: Can you give an example of how God uses spiritual gifts to warn us concerning the devil's tactics?
Answer: Yes. I was holding a meeting in East Texas in the 1950s toward the close of the Korean War. One night I had something in my spirit. I knew God was speaking to a young man.

I said, "Young man, I see right out in front of you — it's only a step out in front of you — a black wall." (I could see, in the Spirit, a black wall.) I told him, "And once you step into it, you're gone. I don't know what it is — but it's something right out in front of you. I do know this much. If you'll come to this altar and give your heart to Jesus, you'll be saved and never go into that darkness." That young man didn't come. The pastor even talked to him, but he wouldn't come.

The next week, while holding a meeting about 100 miles away, I got a letter from the pastor.

He said, "Brother Hagin, I thought you'd be interested in knowing this. The young man whom you said was going into darkness went out and got drunk. He thought he was going home, but he went into the wrong house. He began slamming, hammering and knocking on the door. He tore the screen door off and kicked the door in.

"The man of the house didn't know who was there. He unloaded both barrels of a shotgun right in the boy's face."

This pastor said, "I went to the hospital and the boy was still alive. The doctors didn't understand how he had lived, and they knew he wouldn't live long.

"I talked to him and told him who I was. You couldn't look at him, it was so pitiful. But somewhere down in his throat, I heard these words come out of him: 'Oh, why didn't I listen! Why, oh why, didn't I listen? I couldn't see this darkness out in front of me, but I could feel it. If I had listened to God, I wouldn't have been drunk. If I had listened to God, I wouldn't have been out there . . . .' And then he lapsed off and never did say anything else."

The poor fellow went out into eternity. Was it God's fault? No! God tried to get him to stop. God did His best to arrest his attention. But he didn't listen. He had the power to listen. Why didn't God overrule him? Because God doesn't work that way.

Here's another example of spiritual gifts being used to warn believers. In this case, a man was being used unwittingly by the devil. I was preaching in Oklahoma when suddenly one night, the Word of the Lord came to me.

I said, "Now, everybody listen! (There were between 400 and 500 people in the building.) This meeting will not have been over one week until a man who's in this building tonight will fall dead on his front porch — unless he comes to this altar and repents." I knew that in my spirit. I had that revelation.

I said, "The man lives close enough to this church that you could throw a stone from the church and hit his house. He came to the altar during this meeting, and it seemed like he prayed. But he went out afterwards and told some of you, 'That preacher is a fake.' God, tonight, is calling that man to repentance."

The man never did come. I learned later he was out in front of the church laughing after the service. "Boy," he said, "that preacher tried to throw a scare into me, didn't he? But I don't scare that easy."

We closed the meeting on a Thursday night. The following Sunday the pastor called me. He said, "That man fell dead yesterday afternoon on his front porch, just like you said. He lived within a stone's throw of the church."

Some people, in spite of everything God does, run over every bridge and sign and everything God puts up, and go right on to hell.

Question: Have you ever cast out demons that were manifesting in someone's home?

Answer: Yes, I was holding a meeting for a pastor and his wife almost 20 years ago, and they invited me to their home. Both of them were ministers of the Gospel.

As we were sitting there talking, the wife said, "Brother Hagin, I don't know how to say this to you, but this house we're living in has manifestations of evil spirits."

I don't know why she didn't do something about it. She had the authority. She just didn't know it.

The pastor (he was one of the top men in his Full Gospel denomination) would hear the evil spirits go through the house and knock things over. His wife said, "I've actually spoken to one and it's spoken back to me. I've told it to go and it didn't."

I said, "I'll take care of that for you."

"Will you?" they asked. "We've thought about moving."

"No," I said. "I'll take care of it. You won't ever see or hear these manifestations again in the Name of Jesus."

Just sitting there at the table, speaking in an ordinary conversational tone, I said, "In the Name of Jesus I command every evil spirit to leave, and all demonic activity in this home to cease." I told the couple, "Now it's gone; you'll never hear or see those demons again."

They told me last year — 19 years later — there was never another manifestation of that power. The pastor told me he almost had been embarrassed when his wife had brought the subject up.

But I'm not embarrassed to know the devil and demons are real, are you? They were real in Bible times, and they're just as real now as then. I'm not afraid of them. And you ought not to be — not if you're a Christian, that is.

Question: Are you ever afraid to deal with any case of insanity caused by demons?

Answer: No, I had an unusual experience as a 17 year old that set me free, and it doesn't bother me to deal with any case. Since then I've dealt with seven people right out of mental institutions. Doctors said they would never be any better. Six out of the seven were delivered, and the seventh may have been — I just haven't heard.

This experience I had as a young man happened as I was walking down a street in my home town. Something suddenly came down on me. The best I can describe it, it was a big black something and all the houses took on a different look. I didn't know where I was. I felt like running and screaming and pulling my hair. Something said, "You're going to wind up in the asylum."

But I said, "No you don't, devil, *in the Name of Jesus!*" Thank God for that Name. I said, "In the Name of Jesus, you leave me!" It was right there three feet in front of me. I could not see it, but it was still real.

Well, that thing left me. The houses took on the right kind of look. I said, "Now you go right on and leave me alone, in the Name of Jesus."

The thing backed off. It got far enough away that it didn't bother me. But as I walked on down the street a few feet and got my mind *off* the Lord and *on* something else, suddenly it came down again. It was as if a sack had dropped over my head. I didn't know where I was. Every house took on a funny look. It seemed like my hair stood straight up on top of my head.

I wanted to start running down the street screaming and pulling my hair, and if I had, I would have been completely gone. Something said, "You're going to wind up in the asylum."

Again I said, "Oh no you don't, devil! No, you don't in Jesus' Name!" And he left. I had that same experience three times. And after the third time it never came back.

The Name of Jesus is just as powerful as the person of Jesus. The Name of Jesus can do everything He did when He was here. Thank God we don't have to fear the devil.

Question: Did you ever cast the devil out of a violently angry person?

Answer: Yes, and it takes the boldness, authority, and power of God. You can't do anything within yourself. The Church is a supernatural Church with supernatural equipment, with a supernatural God, a supernatural Jesus, and a supernatural Holy Spirit.

I was holding a meeting in St. Louis once and was ministering to the sick by the laying on of hands. A couple came by in the healing line. The woman was in a wheelchair and her husband was pushing her. He could hardly walk himself (he had arthritis, or something like that). But he also had a devil in him.

I laid hands on the woman first. Her husband was standing beside her, and his eyes flashed fire. He jumped forward and began to curse me violently.

I grabbed both of his wrists and pushed him up against a wall. I made him look at me. He looked away. I said, "No! You look me right in the eye!"

You see, the devil doesn't like to have his bluff called. I made that man look me right in the eye. I got my nose almost up against his nose. I said, "Now, come out of him! Come out of him! In the Name of Jesus, COME OUT OF HIM!" And that devil came out.

After the meeting that fellow was smiling, and he continued smiling the rest of the week.

We need to have supernatural services — and not play church. It all comes about by prayer.

Question: Once you've been delivered, how can you make sure you keep that deliverance?

Answer: After a person gets delivered, he needs to change his ways — his lifestyle — his thinking. Even Christians need to change a lot of times. If you keep on thinking like you were thinking, the devil will come right back. This may sound strange to you, but it's absolutely the truth. *Sometimes after people are healed or delivered, I know they will wind up worse than they were to begin with.*

How do I know? They are still speaking negatively or

thinking wrongly. They will wind up in the same mess they were to begin with, or worse.

It is a fact that the devil will try to come back. He's here. That's his job. I wish you could get Christians to be as faithful on their jobs as the devil is on his.

To stay delivered, people need to read the Bible. They need to depart from evil and do good. They need to walk in close fellowship with God through the Word and through daily prayer.